FACING TROUBLEMAKERS

NOTES ON DEALING WITH CONFLICT

AMR MUNEER DAHAB

authorHOUSE®

AuthorHouse™
1663 Liberty Drive
Bloomington, IN 47403
www.authorhouse.com
Phone: 833-262-8899

Published by AuthorHouse 10/14/2020

ISBN: 978-1-6655-0466-9 (sc)
ISBN: 978-1-6655-0465-2 (e)

Library of Congress Control Number: 2020920332

Print information available on the last page.

To electrical engineering: a bitter life-mate that inspired me in a tough way.

CONTENTS

PREFACE

This book was not written with the purpose of waving a magic wand and crowning you with victory in every single conflict. *Facing Troublemakers* was written to provide you with ideas that inspire you not only with business conflicts but in dealing with life's problems overall.

The book is not only a result of my own experiences but also my observations of conflicts around me, whether at work or in day-to-day life.

Facing Troublemakers is intended to be your gateway to creating your own philosophy for confronting conflicts, discovering your strengths, and overcoming obstacles.

BEFORE WE START

1

▦ Thoughts are for inspiration; rules are for memorizing.

▦ The best way to get the most of this book—any book, really—
is to see how far it inspires you, rather than counting the new
ideas you memorize.

▦ Dealing with conflicts is not a necessity for good people only;
everyone needs to manage his conflicts, whether he is the
initiator or when someone else pushes him into trouble.

▦ Accordingly, if creating conflicts is one of your techniques in
life or business, you will still find this book useful when facing
an expert conflict creator.

▦ You and your opponents might read the same books and join
similar training courses. It is not about who reads the book
first or passes the training with higher marks; it is all about
who gets better inspired.

▦ If you believe the ideas in this book are hard to adopt, do not
worry, you can use them partially and even occasionally.

WHY CONFLICTS EXIST

2

⊞ Conflicts exist in nature, not just human nature.

⊞ Conflicts don't necessarily exist because bad people are present; they exist because different-natured people are present.

⊞ Boredom seems to be one of the most challenging conflict exciters. People tend to search for dynamic situations even when they pass a serene luxuriant long-lasting experience.

⊞ Jealousy mostly comes first among agitated feelings between colleagues.

⊞ As a rule, conflicts do not rise suddenly; they are accumulations of ignored minor disputes or minor differences in views.

⊞ Claiming to reach a final resolution for conflicts sounds like claiming to answer the eternal question of the secret of life. Try to jump over conflicts; life looks like continuous cycles of hurdle races.

CONFLICT EXCITERS AND FAVORITE PLACES

3

- Discrepancies of interests, as well as aggressive people, are major conflict motivators. Boredom looks like an innocent motive but is no less dangerous when behind conflicts.

- Even though they are mostly not driven by good intentions, conflicts are often chances to boost levels of competence in work environments.

- In social life more than in business, critical conflicts can be an introduction to strong and trustworthy relationships, if they occur with people newly introduced to our lives, whereas they are probably fatal to old relationships.

- Conflicts tend to have favorite times and situations rather than favorite places.

- Even the material and moral products that give us relaxation, pleasure, and peace of mind are born from conflict in one way or another.

◈ Contrary to what we tend to believe, conflicts have chances to appear equally at home, in the community, within the neighborhood, at work, and even in a place of worship.

◈ The significance of conflicts depends on the extent to which they affect us and the size of the audience interested in following the show.

◈ It is wise to plan to minimize future conflicts and reduce their negative impact. Planning to stop future conflicts or absolutely avoid them is an impossible mission.

◈ Principles tend to be attractive to unpretentious people; it is exceptional to adhere to your principles when you are in a position of power.

ALLIES

4

- Old, stable relationships can be reliable sources of alliances; just be careful of changes that affect people over time.

- Try your best to cautiously select your allies from among your trustworthy relationships. However, do not stop looking seriously for new, reliable allies; they will be the time-tested relationships of your future.

- When searching for new allies, accurately calculate your needs and interests, as even minor miscalculations could lead to fatal results.

- Cracks in your relationships affect you sharply; negative surprises from alliances can wound you deeply.

- Betrayal is a big word; it is probably not applicable to transient allies' letdowns.

- It does not require a high degree of intelligence to spot a two-faced ally—he exposes himself spontaneously; just be attentive to naive gestures.

▦ Two-faced alliance is not a characteristic only of bad people. Some good people might not be sure of which side to take throughout a conflict. Monitor everyone carefully, and do not take it personally.

▦ Do not wait until you are in the middle of a conflict; make strong ties with potential allies in advance.

▦ Records of past conflicts are a useful tool in selecting your trustworthy allies. However, always keep your eyes open to update your list of allies.

▦ Beware of times your opponents show sudden kindness and when your allies repeat unsolicited confirmations of loyalty.

▦ Declaring that you do not trust anyone is not enough to prove that you are attentive and cautious. Keep a list of your allies categorized by level of trustworthiness.

▦ You are stronger when you are able to declare that you trust more people.

▦ It is your sole responsibility to maintain your image during the conflict and negotiations; do not expect others to defend every minor attack. The support of allies should be reserved for essential, critical turns along your conflict journey.

▦ It is always good to try to anticipate the expiry dates of your allies.

▩ Opponents do not betray you—beware of your allies.

▩ Trust is an important criteria while selecting your allies. However, you need to be smart to identify whom you should trust.

▩ Trusted people are not necessarily your loved ones but those who have the required knowledge and experience and had a good history with you.

NEGOTIATIONS

5

- Before you take on negotiations, make sure you are the right negotiator. Otherwise, delegate another colleague and propose yourself for another possible mission.

- Gather your allies before the negotiation, and try to increase them among the participants while the negotiation is going on.

- When it is your turn to speak, perform as if you are the star of the show and the stage is yours.

- Do not underestimate other people's intelligence when presenting fake concessions; this is the time that you need to be more careful.

- More intelligence, power, and courage are needed if you intend to violate others' rights for tactical or strategic reasons. You have an outstanding status of power to start from when you represent your rights.

- Before negotiating for your rights, make sure your opponents are aware that these are your rights, even if they do not admit so.

▦ Do not offer your final proposals as ultimatums; however, your tone should sound decisive.

▦ Even if you are not satisfied with the outcome, look at it as "less loss"—there could have been further damages.

▦ Although negotiations are meant for resolving conflicts, they could be utilized for further complications or even creating additional conflicts.

▦ After trying all possible proactive approaches, it is okay to put forth your complication plan when you are pushed to a negotiation that you are not interested in or where your opponents seem to have the upper hand.

▦ Your complication plan looks acceptable when it is prepared smartly and presented calmly.

▦ Prepare your renunciations list well ahead, and let it be long enough to allow you to select among several comfortable choices. Make sure to slowly and carefully expose the items one by one, and always keep in mind that the goal is to finalize the negotiations while keeping as many items as possible intact within that list.

▦ It is essential before going in depth with negotiation to identify who wears the good guy hat and who wears the bad guy hat, even though both could be the opposite outside the meeting room.

▦ Even if you are negotiating for yourself or your organization, try to imagine that you are negotiating for somebody else or another party who hired you as a delegate for the mission. This allows you to act enthusiastically and react calmly.

▦ In the next session of a negotiation, try to bring encouraging rewards for your opponents and surprise them with additional challenges.

▦ When your opponents show greediness, it is better to focus on keeping them occupied with the fear of losing the rewards already offered.

▦ It is important not to stick strictly to familiar strategies. Be flexible throughout the negotiation to allow for absorbing your mistakes, considering the behavior of your opponents, and the reevaluation of your prejudgments on their natures and behaviors.

▦ Try to listen openly and carefully to your opponents during the negotiations while accepting their notes on your weaknesses as if they were gifts.

▦ If you discovered that it is a cunning display of muscle rather than being a process of compromising in good faith, then it is better to stick to your stance even if you are convinced that you are not entitled to what you are fighting for.

◈ No matter the barriers—lack of trust, diehard bargainers, or spoilers—with solid arguments and a patient, calm approach, you could discompose your opponent's position.

◈ With the same solid argumentation and a rational approach, you should be able to maintain an impressive image, regardless of the negotiation tactics adopted by your opponents.

◈ If others have prepared well with many surprises, it is better not only to ask for time to study their proposals but to try to keep them busy with your own well-prepared surprises.

BEFORE FALLING INTO
THE CONFLICT TRAP

6

⊞ Before getting into the details of a conflict, reevaluate your position; maybe you could find a way to withdraw without any loss before the battle starts.

⊞ Many conflicts could be won without participating. Think carefully before making the decision to get involved. It may not always be that others have bad intentions; you might be dragged into the wrong conflict by mistake.

⊞ During the harbingers of the conflict, the question is not always how to avoid it. It could be wise to go into the conflict for a radical solution that was previously inaccessible.

⊞ Before getting involved in the conflict, you have the privilege of thinking freshly outside the box. However, you still see neither the details nor the whole picture of the conflict.

⊞ Beware of those who incite you to be a hero; nobody other than you should determine the level of your involvement in the conflict.

▨ Unless you are too busy, do not hesitate to accept an invitation to participate in a relevant conflict as an observer. It is at least a good chance to get some useful information and experience; just maintain your marginal position throughout the process.

▨ Transferring the problem to someone else is more effective before you are trapped in the conflict. However, it is still possible during all phases of the conflict.

▨ Whenever a new conflict emerges, take some time to conduct an independent overview, and then look over your record on past conflicts to review lessons you learned and to get inspired.

▨ When you receive an invitation to a conflict, make sure that you are not in front of a problem transferred to you by someone else.

UNDERSTANDING CONFLICTS

7

◉ Rather than being unique each time, conflicts are mostly recurring events in different forms.

◉ Unlike school days, it is not all about memorizing lessons and scoring high on the examination paper. In practical life, be watchful of conflicts. Keep your head up and look around.

◉ Dealing with conflicts is much more like hurdle races: it is always about how to jump the hurdles better and faster, not removing hurdles from your way while running.

◉ People using the techniques of hurdles racers are more likely to be successful in dealing with conflicts than those using the techniques of short-distance racers.

◉ Our opponents are gifts presented to us for discovering our mistakes and weaknesses and refining our will.

◉ Persistence and perseverance are of the most powerful common tools in dealing with conflicts. Yet, smartness and calmness are not less important by any means.

- In conflicts it goes as in medicine: prevention is better than cure. Keep an eye on your healthy, intact relationships.

- Getting disturbed by conflicts should never stop you from utilizing relevant lessons learned.

- Always try to be ethical. However, when deciding to transfer the conflict to someone else, assure to select the proper victim carefully.

- Negotiations during conflicts are essential for all parties, not necessarily to eliminate the disputed points; negotiations are essential to convince each other jumping to the next hurdle with any kind of consent.

- A diet that encourages you to lose twenty pounds in a month is useless if you are not taught how to maintain your weight loss over the long term. You must train continuously on jumping over conflicts.

- Life is apparently more exciting than a hurdle race. It is better not to expect conflicts to be well organized; they might appear suddenly and in different shapes and volumes.

- Waiting for a conflict to resolve itself is generally not an encouraged idea. Timely avoidance could be a proactive approach. However, avoidance time is relative, depending on each case

- ❖ Conflicts that you are trying to manage are opportunities to expect other unforeseen conflicts and minimize their possible effects.

- ❖ Preemptive actions are always advantageous—why wait for a conflict to start and then wonder about how to deal with it?

- ❖ The worst-case scenario in any conflict is much less than a threat, if you have reasonable alternatives.

- ❖ Being ready for the worst-case scenario, and showing your opponent that you are ready, enhances your position to jump easier and faster over the conflict's hurdles.

- ❖ It is better to reach a win-win situation even if you have the chance to win alone. This enhances trust during future conflicts.

- ❖ It is not easy to identify which is better: a wise opponent or a precipitate one. However, identifying the nature of your opponent is essential in helping you face him better.

- ❖ While implementing conflict management strategies to minimize the negative sides of a conflict and to enhance the positive aspects, the opposite could happen. Reassess the situation continuously, and never trust rules blindly.

- ❖ Your manager's support is essential, and your colleagues' stands are not less important.

⌘ If you totally fail to define the reasons other parties raise during the conflict, firing back would be a proper tactic as long as you fully control your weapons.

⌘ While it is good to take proactive steps anticipating probable future conflicts, it is better not to overact, as that could instigate inexistent conflicts.

⌘ Spend time searching for trustworthy people more than trying to beware doubtful ones.

⌘ You cannot focus on the details and the outline at the same time.

⌘ Conflicts are not areas of appreciation. Do not lose your firmness whatever it takes. Your opponents will try to utilize all the tools at their disposal, including belittling and humiliating others.

⌘ Assure to keep your self-esteem and appreciation of others away from being affected by the conflict outcomes.

⌘ With careful concessions, you could avoid losing potential allies and even turn some of opponents' supporters to your side.

⌘ In conflicts, things go as in football matches. Never start celebrating your victory before you hear the end whistle from the referee.

PRIORITIZING YOUR CONFLICTS

8

⊠ Classification of conflicts priorities is a personal judgment; nobody is better accountable than you about priorities in dealing with your conflicts.

⊠ Still, it is a good idea to get advice from trusted people around you.

⊠ Avoid letting your opponents set your conflicts priorities; this could happen either when you slow down or when you rush in your reactions toward concurrent conflicts.

⊠ Like an examination paper, it is better to start with the easiest-solved conflict.

⊠ Frequently reevaluating your conflicts priorities is a useful tool to enhance your overall performance dealing with conflicts. This might help you eliminate inactive conflicts from your pending list.

⊠ You do not need to worry about their prioritization; urgent conflicts do not fit in your "conflicts to solve" waiting list.

IT IS ALWAYS YOUR OWN WAY

9

◈ It is not only philosophers who have their own way of living; everybody does. Similarly, you do not need to be an expert to have your own approach to deal with conflicts.

◈ When you attempt to eliminate or reduce conflicts (conflict resolution), you might lose the chance of getting use of a conflict. When you attempt to benefit from reasonable levels of conflicts (conflict management), you might hurt yourself underestimating the criticality of a conflict. Assure always to make your own tailor-made evaluation for each conflict.

◈ Win-lose negotiations, win-win negotiations, conflict management, conflict resolution, and others are examples. You do not necessarily need to follow any approved method or technique in negotiations or dealing with conflicts; you are free to create your own ideas.

◈ You will be able to create your approach, or at least use your own interpretation of known methods, if you genuinely desire to win a negotiation or overcome a conflict. Believe deeply in yourself.

◈ You are probably aware of many typical negotiations and conflict controlling techniques; you just happen to give them other names or even utilize them without naming them.

◈ Do not just focus on overexerting your mind memorizing every single reference you had read on the topic.

◈ Being good with everybody is a difficult mission; it is impossible in the long run. Your opponents will not give you this privilege. However, it is worthy to try having relationships that benefit all.

◈ Try to find somebody trustworthy. He must be around you: a manager, a colleague, or a subordinate.

◈ It is worthy to work hard on neutralizing opposing peers, regardless of the level of their involvement in the conflict.

◈ You could still control your conflicts away using the famous tactic "divide and conquer." However, people tend to divide themselves spontaneously, allowing you to rule them your own way.

◈ You need to have your own style of living before you can figure out the best way to deal with conflicts.

◈ Trying to apply tactics and strategies of conflict management and resolution is not a bad idea when you are starting your career. However, in the long run, digest these tactics and strategies, and even forget them, to allow your own thoughts to rise up.

⊗ The right criteria to judge any approach is to see how useful it is when applied practically. Yet do not rush to conclude the invalidity of any approach subsequent to the first practical failure.

⊗ The striking success of a useful tool in a specific situation does not guarantee the repetition of a similar success in different or even apparently similar situations.

⊗ When you target others, you need to carefully study the appropriate approach to be used. When others target you, you will be more confident to impose your own approach; nevertheless, do not assume they have not studied you carefully before deciding to attack.

⊗ Give others the chance for positive feelings toward you. Instead of the classic piece of advice on complimenting others, you could offer better relief to your competing peers by talking about some of your irrelevant personal deficiencies.

REWARDING YOUR OPPONENT

10

- It is not always about winning the current battle; a win-win concept could accommodate a behavior such as a concession of a minor conflict to enhance your chances of winning the next major conflicts.

- Try to think about concession of a minor conflict as a reward given to your opponent, helping him rationalize his loss in an upcoming major conflict.

- In conflicts of interests, and especially when you are clearly the weakest party, try to create interest for your opponents.

- Do not hesitate to offer your opponents preferences that are clearly not going to harm your stance.

- Value your opponents' smartness, and avoid offering fake rewards.

- Enjoying seeing frustration on other people's faces is petty; do not consider it a victory.

- Accepting your opponent's rewards helps boost levels of trust. However, do not allow your opponents overestimate their rewards.

IN THE MIDDLE OF THE CONFLICT

11

▣ It is a good idea to frequently have a refreshing look outside the conflict arena; that helps discover the motivations of your opponents and inspires you for a fresh restart.

▣ In conflict management, an avoiding style ignores the problem, hoping it will go away. This is a useful defensive tool; just beware to hold it the right way at the right time.

▣ During the conflict, you will see only one enemy: your opponent. Other people will look like angels. Actually, they are not, but it is okay to consider them so, at least temporarily.

▣ Avoid misevaluating or underestimating your peers and opponents just because you do not like them.

▣ Try to pay high attention to your opponents' divide-and-conquer tactics. It is important not to lose any of your team members even if you discovered some of their mistakes during the conflict.

▣ Knowledgeable alliances are important, and loyal supporters are significant, but do not forget to have always vital people with positive energy around you during the conflict.

◈ Avoidance style and a wait-and-see attitude are useful only when you become helpless; do not attempt to adopt such approaches proactively.

◈ Claiming lack of understanding is a temporary tool to use when you need more time to think about your opponent's surprises. It is better to show other parties your brainpower all the times.

◈ When your opponent raises the conflict to satisfy a third party, try to find a shortcut to the third party.

◈ Over-trust leads to betrayal pains; over-doubt leads to dilemma.

◈ To overcome your pride and sense of injustice when you find yourself at the end of a conflict with no supporters, it is useful to carry out a feasibility study calculating what you might lose more by continuing to refuse accepting the outcomes of the conflict for the benefit of your opponents.

TO ATTACK OR NOT TO ATTACK?

12

- Even if you feel that you are severely oppressed, do no attempt to fight unless you assure that you are fully prepared and equipped.

- Attack is not always the best means of defense. The best means of defense is the success of throwing illusion into others' minds that you are impenetrable. This is not achievable by magic; it needs lots of smart, hard work.

- Your attack tactics are more efficient when presented embedded within a defense petition.

- Do not worry about your good image being impacted for being the attacker. It is all about how to show your stance and how you are filing your case in front of an eager audience.

- You should never be hesitant whether you decided to initiate the attack or maintain a defensive strategy.

- A counterattack seems essential, yet it is not a must at all time. You could continue dragging your opponent for more mistakes to absorb his strategic inventory of energy.

◈ More dangerous than troublemakers' attacks is their hidden actions to drag you for attacking.

◈ In conflicts, mastering the goalkeeper's role is more important than mastering the striker's.

◈ Regardless of the level of evilness or bad intention by the opponents, conflicts are sometimes escalated by proactive defensive measures taken due to our doubtful overthinking and overestimations.

FACE-TO-FACE WITH TROUBLEMAKERS

13

- Troublemakers do not necessarily initiate problems. However, they are eager to escalate issues in all cases.

- With troublemakers, it is not always a dispute on good and evil definitions. Mostly, they know it and enjoy playing the role of devil in life.

- A dangerous troublemaker is not assessed by his smartness; his danger is estimated by the smashing effects he could achieve.

- A troublemaker colleague is sometimes better than a peaceful fellow, if you could win over that troublemaker as a friend or at least as a partner. It takes hard work to achieve that.

- Do not be surprised if your manager is not taking action against a mischievous colleague. A bad coworker is not necessarily a bad subordinate.

- The traits you do not like could be the strength points of your opponents.

- It is not enough not to let your opponent smell your fear; you must not be frightened.

▨ The strong or even aggressive character is not enough to win a conflict. Do not get disturbed by your opponent's sharp tone and resilient attitude, and present yourself confidently.

▨ You do not need to worry about not identifying the source of power of troublemakers. Just defend your points consistently avoiding unnecessary criticism of other parties.

▨ Waiting for a quarrelsome colleague to leave the organization will not help solving relevant conflicts necessarily, the replacement could be worse.

▨ Before showing your muscles, you need to be sure that you have ones. Just be careful assuring that you are using the right muscles with the right opponent.

▨ In front of a quarrelsome coworker, it is eventually a matter of patience.

▨ Your opponent would be left alone if you could fulfil his manager's expectations.

▨ People throwing negative energy are easily detectable; beware of those who smartly absorb your positive energy.

▨ It is worthy to spend time detecting silent troublemakers.

▨ More dangerous than silent troublemakers are troublemakers who portray themselves as innocent.

◈ Before hiring a troublemaker to fight for you, ensure that he would be under your full control.

◈ Nothing would tease a troublemaker better than a careless response. However, be ready for his following overdrawn reactions.

◈ Resolving conflicts is nothing but destroying a troublemaker's natural environment. Take care when attacking others' comfort zones.

◈ Contrary to what peaceful people might think, troublemakers are not trouble experts; they get annoyed when things do not meet their expectations.

◈ Whenever you suffer in the middle of a conflict, remember that your opponent is suffering as well.

◈ Troublemakers tend to appreciate power and only power; you might show your kindness as needed just for tactical purposes.

◈ Annoyance is not an irregular feeling during conflicts. However, you should never let others feel that you are irritated.

◈ Troublemakers might be smart; they bypass logical concepts in discussion deliberately. Do not waste your energy fetching logical evidences; instead, focus on being smarter and more persistent.

▨ It is not only that your opponent should not realize your unease; you should refresh yourself if your unease lasted quite long during the conflict.

▨ Troublemakers focus on gathering alliances before and throughout the conflict. Do not stand with arms folded in front of them; form your own alliances with smart, strong, and trustworthy people.

▨ Understanding the motivations of the troublemaker is important. However, focusing on the problem itself helps you overcome it better than focusing on the troublemaker.

▨ Troublemakers are not only smart problem creators fighting for themselves; they offer their services as trustworthy allies for current or even expected conflicts.

▨ Contrary to the common impression, a troublemaker could be a silent, calm person. Yet that is not enough to judge whether this kind of troublemakers is more dangerous or less threatening than a loud one.

▨ Troublemaking is a nature; however, it can be gained. The toughest challenge is to turn a genuine troublemaker into a peaceful person.

▨ Besides providing a toxic environment, troublemaking is a profession for some people.

▩ Troublemakers are not always good attackers; they are rather good teasers in their attacking and defending positions.

▩ You owe troublemakers thanks as they offer you free practical lessons on how to deal with other troublemakers.

BECOMING A TROUBLEMAKER

14

⊠ At times, you might have no choice other than creating some obstacles when you believe that the conflict is going toward a resolution that is against your interests.

⊠ You could still be an ethical troublemaker by not creating obstacles unless others are violating your rights, and approaching a conflicted, unhappy ending for you.

⊠ Do it carefully, as while trying to enhance the skills of a newcomer to the work environment dealing with conflicts, he might exceed your expectations, revealing his hidden talent as a troublemaker.

⊠ Whether deliberately or accidently, you cannot create a troublemaker from scratch. A genuine troublemaking nature just awaits a suitable chance to reveal itself.

⊠ Do not only avoid the excitement of becoming a troublemaker unnecessarily. Avoiding to overact during your stubborn positions, even when you believe you are absolutely right, probably deserves more attention from you.

⊗ Troublemakers with strong personalities are inspirational; beware of getting affected by their troublemaking tendency, and focus on their influential approaches.

⊗ Do not try hard to refute the allegations when someone accuses you of troublemaking. Instead, work hard and smartly on having the best of that reputation.

⊗ Being surrounded by troublemakers at any level helps spread the infection to you. If you are stuck in such forced relationships, assure to get fresh air frequently by forcing yourself to take periodic breaks with prudent fellows.

15

ETHICS CHALLENGES

◈ The greatest challenge with ethics is the definition itself.

◈ Being ethical can make you feel as if you are in continuous conflicts. Stick to your ethics, but beware of exhausting yourself fighting windmills.

◈ Although conflicts are quite often referred to as war, it is good to stick to your values even if others do not show you their esteem. People regularly evaluate and admire your performance, even if they rarely express their admiration.

◈ Do not exaggerate the fear of getting your hands dirty while you are trying to overcome conflicts ethically.

◈ Even if you are a good person, you will recognize that playing conflicts ethically is not your independent decision. Nevertheless, that does not mean you should extend your hands completely to the devil.

◈ Before refuting your opponent's false claims about you, think whether they can be exploited to your advantage without admitting them.

⊞ Your opponent may provide false claims that benefit both of you in front of the media and the public. This is a win-win situation but not absolutely when you play ethically.

⊞ It is not always a tricky approach; transferring the problem is a must when you realize it originally pertains to others, or at least should be shared with other concerned parties.

⊞ When you fight ethically, that decreases your chances to win. However, you can still turn the situation in your favor by confirming your opponent's suspicions that you are just playing the ideal opponent's role.

⊞ Revenge should be your last motive, and it is better to eliminate it from your motivations list. This probably allows you to think and act wisely and efficiently.

⊞ Accepting the following fact does not mean that you are necessarily bypassing ethics: your current opponent could be your next ally, and vice versa.

⊞ Be careful of your own tactics and strategies; it is a fine line between what you consider legitimate tricks and betrayal.

⊞ Sometimes it looks even like a gray area; consider your trustworthy coworker's evaluation if your action is perceived by others as betrayal.

⊞ Winning the conflict depends on how you deliver your case, more than being right or wrong. That doubles your ethics challenges.

RECURRENCE OF CONFLICTS

16

◈ History repeats itself, but not with every single detail.

◈ When you face the same conflict again with the same people, scrutinize your mistakes from dealing with the conflict last time.

◈ When the same conflict is repeated with the same people involved, reevaluate their attitude; it could be the same faces with an entirely different behavior.

◈ Reassess yourself frequently; you are changing as well.

◈ When the same conflict is repeated with different people involved, you should better consider it as a new conflict necessitates a new approach.

◈ Conflict recurrence does not necessarily mean you are responsible.

◈ In many cases, a specific conflict does not actually reoccur; you just thought the conflict reached an end while it was still ongoing, maybe behind the scenes.

▩ We often tend to put our conflicts on hold and then become annoyed when they flare up again after a while.

▩ Even your past conflicts might not be enough to remind you when a similar conflict happened before. Do not be bothered by your weak memory; just focus on realizing the value of your subconscious and your rich stock of inspiration.

▩ Annual challenging business tasks are probably prescheduled recurring conflicts. Whenever you memorize lessons learned, be ready for surprises eliminating previous obstacles and adding unexpected new ones.

DEALING WITH BETRAYAL

17

◈ More difficult than gaining trust is regaining it.

◈ Why make the decision to lose somebody? Let the other person take the initiative.

◈ Even if you anticipate it and believe you are prepared in advance, betrayal will still taste harsh when it happens.

◈ In order to avoid getting hurt by others, you do not need to sleep with one eye open—close both eyes while sleeping and keep your mind and heart open when you are awake.

◈ Betrayal is a feeling that people enjoy allowing it to exacerbate. Chances of success overtaking betrayal's frustration increase when we are able to ignore frustrations and look at possible recovery and brilliant opportunities in the future or currently around us.

◈ Bad intention is not the only motive leading to betrayal. Other reasons include misunderstanding, miscommunication, fears, weakness, and genuine needs, among others.

🎑 Betrayal from others needs to be carefully evaluated by you; not every betrayal necessitates breaking off relationships. However, a radical change in the relationship is a must after each betrayal.

🎑 The first betrayal's effects tend to be horrible. It is easier after that, not because you get used to it but because your expectations drop.

🎑 It depends on your nature, but try your best to forget the betrayal and remember lessons learned.

🎑 Do not let the satisfaction of the feeling of the victim of betrayal overwhelm you; this leads to nowhere. Try to look for practical alternatives.

🎑 Reactions to betrayal need profound consideration more than just taking revenge.

DO HAPPY ENDINGS
EXIST IN CONFLICTS?

18

◈ Rather than being eliminated forever, resolved conflicts are transferred to a kind of recycle bin.

◈ Instead of waiting for happy endings, live happily regardless of conflicts; they are an irremovable part of life.

◈ A conflict could have an absolutely happy ending, but that is not the point; it is about how to manage the continuous process of dealing with conflicts, especially when happy endings are the luck of your opponents.

◈ Quitting the job is not a bad decision, but it is better not to take it under the pressure of the existing job conflict.

◈ The best job opportunities do not regularly rise when you are in the middle of a conflict.

◈ You do not need to know more about celebrating a conflict victory, just avoid showing overwhelming joy.

❈ Being prepared to the worst-case scenario is the best way of facing unhappy endings.

❈ Happy endings exist in conflicts, but remember that your conflict's happy ending is your opponent's nightmare, and vice versa.

❈ Rather than hoping a conflict has a happy ending, work smartly and professionally to assure you keep your head up no matter the outcomes of the conflicts.

❈ Losing a conflict is not the end of the world; just do not forget to give this loss a unique name to remind yourself about lessons learned.

❈ Frustration will not help you, so instead congratulate your opponent when he wins; this presents you as a strong loser.

❈ Sometimes both parties feel okay to keep the conflict ongoing at a certain level just to fulfill a psychological need.

❈ A happy ending could happen to some or even most of your conflicts, but definitely not to all of them.

❈ It is not wise to feel sorry so long for an unhappy end of a conflict, considering that conflicts themselves do not reach an end in life.

Printed in the United States
By Bookmasters